Pros and Cons
ENERGY SOURCES
The Impact of Science and Technology

Rob Bowden

Gareth Stevens
Publishing

Please visit our web site at: www.garethstevens.com.
For a free color catalog describing Gareth Stevens Publishing's list of high-quality books, call 1-800-542-2595 (USA) or 1-800-387-3178 (Canada). Gareth Stevens Publishing's fax: 1-877-545-2596

Library of Congress Cataloging-in-Publication Data

Bowden, Rob, 1973-
    Energy sources : the impact of science and technology / by Rob Bowden.
        p. cm. — (Pros and cons)
    Includes bibliographical references and index.
    ISBN-10: 1-4339-1987-7   ISBN-13: 978-1-4339-1987-9 (lib. bdg.)
    1. Power resources—Juvenile literature. I. Title.
TJ163.23.B649   2010
333.79—dc22   2009012434

This North American edition published in 2010 by Gareth Stevens Publishing under license from Arcturus Publishing Limited.
Gareth Stevens Publishing
A Weekly Reader® Company
1 Reader's Digest Road
Pleasantville, NY 10570-7000 USA

Copyright © 2009 Arcturus Publishing Limited
Produced by Arcturus Publishing Limited
26/27 Bickels Yard
151-153 Bermondsey Street
London SE1 3HA

Gareth Stevens Executive Managing Editor: Lisa M. Herrington
Gareth Stevens Editor: Jayne Keedle
Gareth Stevens Senior Designer: Keith Plechaty

Series Concept: Alex Woolf
Editor and Picture Researcher: Nicola Barber
Cover Design: Phipps Design
Consultant: Dr. Robert Fairbrother

CONTENTS

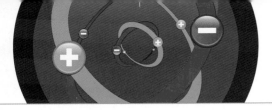

CHAPTER 1

A World of Energy

Everything on Earth depends on energy to survive. Humans need energy from food to stay alive. We also use various forms of energy to warm or cool ourselves, and to move around. Virtually all of the energy used on Earth comes from the Sun. Plants use energy from the Sun to grow, for example. Even the gas we put in our cars can be traced back to the Sun, because it is made from the fossilized remains of plants and animals that lived millions of years ago. Those ancient plants and animals depended on the Sun for energy, and when they died, some of that energy was captured and stored in their remains.

Everlasting Energy

In scientific terms, energy is the ability to do work. Energy cannot be created or destroyed. It can be transformed from one form to another, but the total amount of energy in the universe is always the same. For example, a photovoltaic cell in a solar panel converts radiant energy from the Sun into electrical energy. Your

Forms of Energy

There are many different forms of energy, but they are catagorized into two main groups — kinetic energy and potential energy.

Kinetic energy is the energy of motion. Here are some examples:

● **Radiant energy** is electromagnetic energy that travels in waves. It includes visible light, X-rays, and radio waves. Solar energy from the Sun is an example of radiant energy.

● **Thermal energy** is the internal energy in a substance created by the vibration or movement of molecules. Geothermal energy comes from heat beneath Earth's surface.

● **Motion energy** is the movement of objects from one place to another. Wind is an example of motion energy.

Potential energy is stored energy. Here are some examples:

● **Chemical energy** is the energy stored in the bonds between atoms. The energy stored in oil, coal, or biomass, such as plants, is an example.

● **Gravitational energy** is the energy in an object that is held against the force of gravity. The water in a dam is held against gravity, for example.

● **Nuclear energy** is the energy stored in the nucleus of an atom. It is released when the nucleus is split or joined with other nuclei.

body obtains chemical energy from the food you eat and converts some of it into motion energy to enable you to move.

Energy for Good … and Bad

In the 21st century, people use energy in a wide variety of ways — to power computers, to light and heat homes, to fly across the world, and to manufacture goods. Almost all of that energy comes from fossil fuels, such as coal and oil. The ability to make use of these ancient stores of energy is one of the greatest technological triumphs of all time, but it has downsides too. Fossil fuels will run out one day, and they are already becoming harder to find and more difficult to extract. Burning fossil fuels creates air pollution and has a major impact on the global environment.

Time to Change Direction?

Less damaging sources of energy, such as the Sun, wind, and water were in use long before fossil fuels were discovered. Those renewable resources are now being reconsidered in a bid to prevent further harm to our environment. The technologies to harness that energy are developing rapidly, but face many obstacles. They are more expensive, and the energy sources may be less reliable — the wind does not always blow, for example. More reliable but perhaps more risky technologies, such as nuclear power, could solve that problem. However, the safety concerns and unknown long-term effects make nuclear energy an unpopular choice for many people.

Whatever direction energy takes in the future, science and technology will play a key role in what is possible, affordable, and acceptable. This book explores some of the options and considers the developments in each energy source over recent decades.

Energy is essential for everything we do, from unconscious actions such as breathing to the conscious actions of playing sports such as basketball.

CHAPTER 2

Energy From Fossil Fuels

Most of the energy consumed on Earth comes from the three main fossil fuels — oil, coal, and natural gas. Between them, those fuels accounted for nearly 81 percent of global energy use in 2006. All fossil fuels are made from the remains of plants and animals that died millions of years ago. Over time, those remains became buried under decaying matter. Squashed under layers of sand, clay, and rock, the remains were compressed in very hot conditions until they turned into coal, oil, and natural gas.

Stored Carbon

Fossil fuels contain large quantities of carbon, an element that occurs naturally in our environment. Because of their high carbon content, fossil fuels are a valuable source of energy. Coal, in particular, powered the Industrial Revolution, which started in Great Britain in the late 1700s. As a result of that revolution, engines and machines largely replaced the work done by people and animals.

The process of burning fossil fuels to provide energy releases carbon as carbon dioxide (CO_2). Over the past 200 years, and particularly since the beginning of the 20th century, the buildup of CO_2 emissions has contributed to a warming of the atmosphere, known as global warming.

Global Warming

Global warming is an increase in the average near-Earth atmospheric temperature. Carbon dioxide (CO_2) and other gases act as a blanket around Earth, allowing radiant energy from the Sun to pass through but trapping some of it in Earth's atmosphere. These gases are known as "greenhouse gases," because they trap heat in much the same way a greenhouse does. Greenhouse gases are needed to keep our planet warm. Without them, Earth's average temperature would be about 1 degree Fahrenheit (−17°C), or well below freezing. Since the Industrial Revolution, however, use of fossil fuels and the resulting CO_2 emissions have increased dramatically. The 1990s was the warmest decade since temperature records began in 1861. Many scientists predict that temperatures could increase by 3.2 to 7.1 degrees Fahrenheit (1.8 to 4°C) by 2100.

Scientists have connected global warming to the melting of ice in polar regions, to crops dying because of unusual weather patterns, and to the increased risk of extreme weather.

Unsustainable Fuels

Fossil fuels are spread unevenly around the world, and they are nonrenewable. Once they are gone, they cannot be replaced. That means fossil fuels are an unsustainable source of energy. Experts predict that at current rates of use, accessible and affordable oil supplies will run out in about 2050, natural gas in about 2070, and coal in about 2140.

Heavy traffic pollutes the air in San Francisco, California. Human ingenuity has enabled people to use the energy stored in fossil fuels — but at a cost.

Percentage of Proven Global Reserves of Major Fossil Fuels by Region			
Region	**Oil**	**Coal**	**Gas**
Africa	9.5	5.8	8.2
Asia Pacific	3.3	30.4	8.2
Europe & Eurasia	11.6	32.1	33.5
Middle East	61.0	0.2	41.2
North America	5.6	29.6	4.5
South & Central America	9.06	1.9	4.4

Source: BP Statistical Review of World Energy 2008

Cleaner Coal

Coal is an inexpensive and abundant fuel source that is used by many nations to meet their energy needs. China is currently leading the world in its production of large coal-fired power stations. But coal is a dirty fuel that emits more CO_2 per unit of electricity than either oil or natural gas. Carbon capture and storage (CCS) technologies offer ways to reduce the impact of burning coal. The CO_2 is collected as the coal is burned, and then the gas is pumped into rocks deep below the ground. Empty oil fields are other possible storage sites. CO_2 is already being injected into near-empty wells as a way of forcing out any remaining oil. About 38.5 million tons (35 million tonnes) of CO_2 are injected into U.S. oil wells each year. New coal-fired CCS power stations could capture up to 95 percent of the carbon in coal and dramatically reduce emissions.

Coal at the Jing Hua Gong coal mine in Shanxi, China, is loaded into a truck for transportation to one of China's coal-fired power stations. China's reliance on relatively low-quality coal has made it one of the world's largest emitters of carbon dioxide.

PROS: ENERGY FROM COAL

Carbon capture and storage (CCS) greatly reduces the impact of burning coal on global warming. The storage methods are considered safe and are expected to retain 99 percent of the CO_2 injected into them over 1,000 years. CCS allows the continued use of coal as an inexpensive and widely available fuel.

 CONS: ENERGY FROM COAL

CO_2 emissions are only one of many problems of burning coal for energy. Mining coal is also dangerous and environmentally harmful. It is estimated that in 2005 between 6,000 and 10,000 workers were killed in Chinese coal mines as a result of floods, cave-ins, or explosions. Mining scars the landscape and pollutes the air and water, and the burning of coal releases a wide range of pollutants in addition to CO_2. The biggest problem with coal, however, is that it is nonrenewable and will one day run out or become too expensive to use.

Types of Coal

There are three main types of coal. They vary according to the pressure under which they were formed and how much carbon they contain. Each has different qualities:

- **Lignite** is a dry and crumbly coal, containing only about 50 percent carbon. Also known as brown coal, it gives off the least heat and the most pollution.
- **Bituminous coal** is a harder coal containing more carbon than lignite. It is the most common coal and burns with a good heat, but is still causes pollution.
- **Anthracite** is a very hard, black coal that is about 90 percent carbon. It burns at high temperatures, giving off the most heat and the least pollution.

Energy to Change the World

Oil has changed the world more than any other energy source. It provides people with the fuel to run cars and fly airplanes and is, for many nations, the main fuel for generating electricity. Oil is also the raw material for making many plastics, paints, fertilizers, fabrics, cosmetics, and countless other goods and materials. Oil is normally found in high-pressure wells deep underground. It is released by drilling into the wells from the surface. In places where the pressure is lower, pumps are used to extract the oil, or water, gas, or steam is injected to force the oil to the surface. Over the years, the oil industry has developed technology

The 800-mile (1,287-kilometer) Trans-Alaska Pipeline carries oil from remote regions of Alaska to the port of Valdez. Some people consider projects such as this to be too costly, and say that they endanger habitats and wildlife.

to drill deeper and in more remote locations; for example, at sea where offshore platforms access oil that lies deep beneath the seabed.

The value of oil is so great that it is sometimes referred to as "black gold." It is found only in certain parts of the world, yet it is needed and used worldwide. The Middle East is particularly rich in oil, and that has led to struggles to control the region's reserves. In some areas, the exploration of oil reserves has caused controversy because of its impact on the local environment and wildlife. Proposals to drill for oil in Alaska's Arctic National Wildlife Refuge, for instance, have caused heated debate.

New Oil Technology

With oil supplies running out, oil companies are looking at new technologies to extract oil from unconventional sources. One technology being developed is the extraction of oil from tar sands. The oil is contained in the bitumen, or tar, that makes up about 10 percent of most of those sands, the rest being clay, sand, and water. The bitumen must be separated, using a lengthy and expensive process, and then purified and thinned before it can be used as oil. Tar sands are found in various parts of the world, but their exploitation is most developed in Alberta, Canada, where around one million barrels of oil are produced each day.

New Source, Same Problem

VIEWPOINT

The search for new sources of oil is leading to ever more expensive and elaborate technologies. Many environmentalists question the continued focus on oil-based energy, however, because producing it and using it creates pollution:

"It takes about 29 kilograms [64 pounds] of CO_2 to produce a barrel of oil conventionally. That figure can be as much as 125 kg [275 lbs] for tar sands oil. [Tar sands extraction] also has the potential to kill off or damage the vast forest wilderness [in Canada], greater than the size of England and Wales ...."

(Mike Hudema, Climate and Energy Campaigner, Greenpeace, Canada)

➕ PROS: TAR SANDS EXTRACTION

Oil is a central part of our lives, so finding new ways to continue its production will help sustain modern lifestyles. The technology required to produce oil from tar sands already exists and is improving as more companies become involved. Once the oil is extracted from the tar sands, the remaining sand and clay can be returned to their original site and the landscape reclaimed for other uses.

A miner holds a sample of tar sands at a mine in Alberta, Canada. Canada is a world leader in developing the technology to extract oil from such sands. However, the process is very expensive and could destroy many fragile ecosystems.

CONS: TAR SANDS EXTRACTION

Extracting oil from tar sands uses vast amounts of energy and creates large volumes of waste. It takes about 2 tons (1.8 tonnes) of tar sand to produce just one barrel of oil. Producing a single barrel of oil also requires up to four barrels of water, which is heavily polluted during the separation process. It also uses as much natural gas as it takes to heat an average family home for four to five days. Critics say this process makes extraction a wasteful technology that will never replace conventional oil drilling. They argue that the money being spent on tar sands extraction should be used for renewable energy technologies instead.

Natural Gas

Natural gas is another of the world's major fossil fuels. Its use has increased rapidly in recent decades, mainly because it is cleaner than coal or oil and produces fewer emissions for the same amount of energy. Gas is used to generate electricity, or is piped directly to homes and industries for use as a heating and cooking fuel. The advantage of natural gas is that it produces a high-quality, instant energy. That can also make it dangerous, however. If natural gas is not handled properly, it can be highly explosive. For that reason, gas supplies and gas appliances such as stoves and boilers must be fitted with safety equipment to protect users.

Why Does Gas Smell?

If someone leaves the gas on by mistake, you will probably know by its smell, which is a little like rotten eggs. But natural gas has no smell on its own. The odor is added to the gas supply to make it easier for people to detect a gas leak. Without the smell, gas could leak without anyone knowing, and if gas comes near a source of ignition, such as the spark of a light switch as it is turned on, it can explode. If you ever smell gas, leave the building immediately. Once safely out of the building, call for emergency help.

Making the Most of Natural Gas

Natural gas is normally found underground, often alongside oil. In many regions the oil industry burns off natural gas as a by-product of the drilling process. That is known as flaring, and it is a major contributor to global warming. It also wastes usable natural gas — an estimated 5.29 trillion cubic feet (150 billion cubic meters) per year. The natural gas is burned off largely because of the difficulty and expense of capturing and transporting it.

One solution is to turn the natural gas into liquefied natural gas (LNG). That involves cooling natural gas to about -259°F (-162°C) until it condenses and forms a liquid. LNG is a source of highly concentrated energy that is easier to transport than natural gas, taking up about 600 times less space than its gaseous equivalent. Natural gas from the remotest locations can be converted into LNG and shipped to where it is needed. In 2008, there were about 60 LNG import terminals around the world. Once imported, the LNG is heated to turn it back into a gas.

 PROS: NATURAL GAS

Natural gas gives off fewer emissions than coal or oil. Capturing the natural gas that is currently being released as a waste product of the oil industry could dramatically reduce overall greenhouse gas emissions. LNG technology makes it possible to capture natural gas from even very remote regions. As more countries adopt LNG facilities, the costs of the technology will become more affordable.

 CONS: NATURAL GAS

Natural gas is a nonrenewable energy source and is difficult and expensive to capture and transport. It is potentially explosive if mishandled, and though it produces fewer emissions than coal or oil, it still contributes to global warming by releasing CO_2 when it is burned. LNG technology is encouraging the development of more gas fields, rather than investment in renewable energy alternatives.

Stopping the Waste

International organizations trying to reduce the impact of energy use on climate change have made reducing the waste of natural gas through flaring a priority:

"In a number of countries, regulatory, financial, and infrastructure barriers still hamper the utilization of natural gas associated with oil production. Governments and companies need to cooperate in removing these obstacles and realizing the value of this wasted resource while minimizing the environmental harm caused by gas flaring."

(Somit Varma, World Bank Group's Director for Oil, Gas, Mining, and Chemicals)

Natural gas is burned as a waste product from this oil platform in the North Sea. There is now international agreement to reduce flaring because of its contribution to rising carbon dioxide levels.

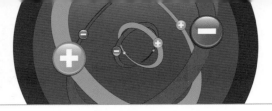

CHAPTER 3

Nuclear Energy

Scientists began to explore the power contained in individual atoms at the start of the 20th century, but it was not until the 1930s that attempts to split the atom to release its energy were successful. After the start of World War II (1939–1945), atomic energy research was largely diverted into the construction of the world's first atomic bomb. In 1945, U.S. planes dropped two atomic bombs on Hiroshima and Nagasaki in Japan, flattening large parts of the cities and killing about 140,000 people. The terrifying power of the bombs ended the war. At the same time, a race began to create commercially usable atomic energy for generating electricity.

Peaceful Power

The world's first commercial atomic power station opened in the United Kingdom in 1956. Today, atomic power is more commonly known as nuclear power. In 2008, 30 countries had operating nuclear power plants that between them generated about 15 percent of the world's electricity. In France, nuclear power accounts for 77 percent of electricity production. Several other countries, including Sweden, South Korea, Ukraine, and Belgium, rely on nuclear energy for more than 40 percent of their electricity.

Nuclear Power Generation

Nuclear power uses a controlled nuclear reaction to heat water to produce steam. The steam drives turbines that turn to generate electricity. The most common fuel, uranium, is processed to make pellets of nuclear fuel. Those pellets are then placed inside metal tubes made of zircaloy, an alloy consisting largely of zirconium. The tubes, called fuel rods, are put together in batches to create a fuel assembly, which is placed inside the nuclear reactor. The uranium in the fuel rods decays and splits — a process known as nuclear fission. Subatomic particles called neutrons are released in that process. Those hit other uranium atoms, releasing more neutrons and causing a chain reaction. Each time an atom is split, it releases energy that is used to heat water for generating electricity.

Nuclear power has the potential to meet our energy needs. As climate change becomes a concern, many countries are looking again at the nuclear option. They are attracted to it because it is a proven technology with high levels of efficiency. Just 1 ton (0.9 tonne) of uranium, for example, will generate the same amount of electricity as about 22,000 tons (20,000 tonnes) of coal or 300 million cubic feet (8.5 million cubic meters) of natural gas. Unlike fossil fuels, nuclear power produces no emissions of carbon dioxide or methane, so it has little effect on global warming.

Uranium fuel pellets are carefully loaded into fuel rods by a technician at the Novosibirsk Chemical Concentrate Plant in Russia. The fuel will be used in nuclear reactors to generate electricity.

Controversial Energy

Nuclear power is one of the most controversial energies in use today. The fear of accidents and the problem of what to do with nuclear waste are both major challenges for the industry. An additional controversy is the association of nuclear materials with warfare and weapons.

Nuclear Dangers

Nuclear materials pose unique dangers. Their use in nuclear power plants produces highly radioactive materials that are hazardous to people and the environment. Radioactive materials emit invisible rays of radiation that can cause damage to living tissues in people, plants, and animals. In humans, that damage is often in the form of cancer. Nuclear power plants are designed to keep the radioactive material contained within the reactor. Even so, some countries have avoided nuclear energy because of fears about the safety of the technology. There have been a number of accidents, notably at Three Mile Island in the United States in 1979, and at Chernobyl in Ukraine in 1986.

Spent fuel from a nuclear reactor is highly radioactive. Some of that nuclear waste can be reused by careful reprocessing (a sort of specialized recycling), but that process creates more highly radioactive waste. Over time, nuclear waste will return to relatively unharmful radiation levels, but scientists believe that could take up to 100,000 years. Keeping nuclear waste safe for such a long period is a major challenge. At the moment, nuclear waste is typically stored by encasing it in glass and putting it in concrete-filled barrels. Scientists are currently testing facilities to store those barrels underground, where they will remain contained for thousands of years until the danger of radiation has passed.

In 1980, exactly a year after the accident at Three Mile Island nuclear power plant, protesters held a candlelight vigil to show their concern about the continuing operation of the plant.

Nuclear Waste

One of the greatest challenges for the nuclear energy industry is how to handle the waste created by the process. There are very different opinions on the importance of this and on how best to handle it:

"People won't accept nuclear power until you deal with waste .... It is a problem that lasts for so long, it becomes a moral issue."

**(Professor Martin Dove,
Cambridge-MIT Institute,
Cambridge, United Kingdom)**

"Nuclear power is the only energy-producing technology which takes full responsibility for all its wastes .... The amount of radioactive wastes is very small relative to wastes produced by fossil fuel electricity generation. Safe methods for the final disposal of high-level wastes are technically proven; the international consensus is that this should be deep geological [underground] disposal."

(World Nuclear Association)

A scientist sits inside a tunnel 2,133 feet (650 meters) below ground in New Mexico. The tunnel is used to store nuclear waste. It is one of many systems being tried out around the world to meet the growing problem of nuclear waste storage.

Nuclear Weapons

The same processes used to make fuel for nuclear power stations can be used to create uranium for weapons. Plutonium, produced as a waste product of the reaction process, can also be used in nuclear weapons. The International Atomic Energy Agency (IAEA) is responsible for monitoring nuclear material use around the world. It inspects power plants regularly and records the movement of materials in and out of them. This is to stop countries from using nuclear materials for purposes of aggression. The IAEA is also concerned about nuclear materials falling into the hands of terrorist organizations that might use them against innocent civilians.

Fission and Fusion

Nuclear fission involves the splitting of atoms to release energy and is the process used in current nuclear power stations. Nuclear fusion is the opposite and releases energy by joining atoms. The Sun is basically a nuclear fusion reactor in which hydrogen atoms collide to form helium and release incredible amounts of energy as a result.

Despite the IAEA's safeguards, Iraq and Iran both managed to develop uranium processing facilities without informing the IAEA. That raised concerns that the facilities were being used to develop weapons, and international pressure was used to close them down. North Korea is also suspected of using nuclear energy facilities to develop weapons. North Korea rarely allows the IAEA to inspect its nuclear facilities, which makes it difficult to monitor what the country is doing.

Nuclear Fusion

Using nuclear fission, or splitting atoms, to produce energy is now a relatively established technology. Most developments in its science focus on alternative reactor models that are smaller, more efficient, and safer, with lower costs and less waste. For most nuclear scientists, the real

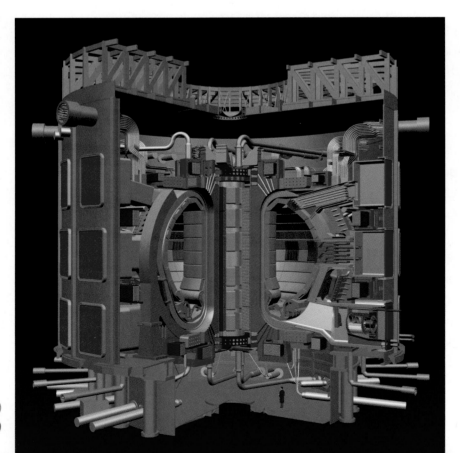

The man (*bottom*) in a computer-generated image of the International Thermonuclear Experimental Reactor (ITER) indicates the size of the reactor. The doughnut-shaped section in the center is where the reaction will take place.

excitement is the possibility of nuclear fusion (joining atoms) — the reaction that occurs in the Sun and the stars. Scientists believe that if they could control fusion reactions on Earth, then they could provide an almost limitless and pollution-free source of energy for the future. The technology has been proven to work in laboratory experiments but has yet to be developed into an affordable and practical technology. Work is currently under way on the International Thermonuclear Experimental Reactor (ITER) in France at a cost of around $10 billion. The reactor is being built by scientists from Russia, Canada, Japan, and Europe. When completed in 2016, it is hoped that the ITER will enable scientists to begin developing the next phase of nuclear energy. The goal is to move from fission reactors to fusion ones by the end of the century.

PROS: NUCLEAR FUSION

Nuclear fusion would use hydrogen atoms from seawater and the common metal lithium, both of which are readily available. Although using lithium would still produce radioactive wastes, these would be much less harmful than wastes from fission reactors and would typically be safe within 100 years. Nuclear fusion would produce no greenhouse gases and could provide large amounts of energy to replace sources that produce more pollution. One clear advantage of nuclear fusion is that it uses a type of fuel that could not be adapted for use in nuclear weapons.

CONS: NUCLEAR FUSION

As of now, nuclear fusion technology has been proven only in a laboratory and is unlikely to become commercially available until the middle of the 21st century. The development costs of nuclear fusion technology are enormous, and there is no guarantee that it will ever be affordable. Some argue that money should instead be spent to advance more proven technologies that harness readily available energy sources, such as the Sun, wind, and water.

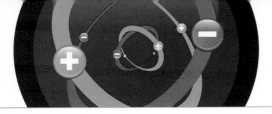

CHAPTER 4

Geothermals and Ambient Energy

In places where Earth's crust, or outermost layer, is thin, there is ample evidence of the vast stores of thermal energy deep beneath the surface of Earth. Volcanic eruptions often send out huge amounts of red-hot rock and gas. Although eruptions are unpredictable and too powerful to offer any useful form of energy, volcanic regions often have more reliable and constant thermal energy. This is in the form of superheated rocks or

In some places on Earth, the thermal energy beneath our feet rises very close to the surface. In Yellowstone National Park, water heated by geothermal energy explodes through holes in the ground. These hot springs are called geysers.

superheated water. Superheating is the process of heating something under pressure to a very high temperature. A substance that is superheated has a lot of stored energy that, if released, can be converted into useful forms. When this energy occurs underground, it is known as geothermal energy. It can be used for direct heating or captured to generate electricity.

The Heat Beneath Our Feet

VIEWPOINT

Scientists are only now developing technologies that could allow us to use the large stores of natural thermal energy below Earth's surface. The technology is still quite expensive, but the possibilities for the future are great:

"Few people know that the heat in the upper six miles [9.6 kilometers] of Earth's crust contains 50,000 times as much energy as found in all the world's oil and gas reserves combined. The potential of geothermal energy to provide electricity, to heat homes and greenhouses, and to supply process heat for industry is vast."

(Time for Plan B, *Earth Policy Institute***)**

Direct Heating

Direct heating uses geothermal energy found beneath the ground to provide heat directly for use in buildings. The geothermal energy is normally transferred using a large-scale commercial heat exchanger. That device transfers heat from one source to another to heat water for an entire district. It is known as a district heating system. In the Icelandic capital, Reykjavík, 95 percent of buildings are heated by water that is piped from beneath the ground at a temperature of 187°F (86°C) into a district heating system. Similar systems operate in the United States, Sweden, New Zealand, and France to provide direct heat energy from geothermal sources. In Klamath Falls, Oregon, a direct heating system installed under the roads provides an additional function by stopping them from freezing over in the winter. Direct geothermal systems are also used to heat soils in greenhouses and to warm ponds used for fish breeding.

Geothermal Electricity

Geothermal energy can be used to heat water and produce steam for driving turbines to generate electricity. In some locations superheated steam can be used directly from the ground to power turbines. Where temperatures are lower, the geothermal source is used in a heat exchanger. The geothermal energy is used to heat a liquid with a lower boiling point than water. As the liquid vaporizes, it drives a turbine. In 2008, the electricity from geothermal plants provided electricity for around 2.8 million homes in the United States.

Ground Source Heat Pumps

Large geothermal installations such as district heating are expensive and only practical on a large scale. Ground source heat pumps are an example of geothermal energy that can be used on a smaller scale. No matter what the surface temperature, about 10 feet (3 meters) below ground the temperature averages 50°F to 61°F (10°C to 16°C). That constant temperature can be used to heat homes in cold weather and to remove heat in hotter conditions. The system works by connecting a heat exchanger to pipes that are buried either vertically or horizontally below the ground. The pipes draw on the thermal energy below ground and pass it into a domestic heating system through the heat exchanger. In hot weather, the system can work in reverse and take heat away from buildings by exchanging it for cooler air from underground.

Ground source heat pumps require electricity to operate, but they are still highly efficient —

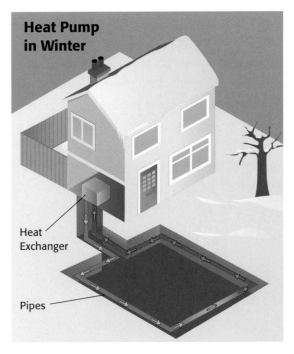

Heat Pump in Winter

Heat Exchanger

Pipes

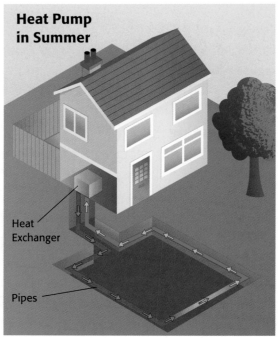

Heat Pump in Summer

Heat Exchanger

Pipes

These diagrams show how a simple ground source heat pump can help to meet the heating and cooling needs of a typical home. Using heat pumps reduces the need for energy from nonrenewable sources.

especially if the electricity to power them comes from renewable sources such as solar or wind power. This technology is already well used in the United States and Scandinavia, and is becoming more popular. Once the system has been installed, the running costs are low and can lead to savings on heating and cooling bills. Prices for other fuels, such as oil and gas, have risen dramatically in recent years, but underground heat is free.

 PROS: GROUND SOURCE HEAT PUMPS

Ground source heat pumps reduce the use of other sources of energy and cut bills at the same time. The technology is well developed and requires very little maintenance, which makes it cheap to run after the initial installation costs. One of the major benefits of this geothermal energy is that the supply is constant and does not fluctuate, unlike solar or wind technologies, which are both affected by constantly changing weather conditions.

 CONS: GROUND SOURCE HEAT PUMPS

Heat pumps require a lot of available space below ground. Because of that, the technology is of little use for high-density housing such as apartments, unless more expensive district systems are used. Ground source heat pumps are useful only for heating rooms and for partially warming water. Additional energy is needed to generate electricity, to raise water to temperatures that are high enough for use in bathing, and to supplement space heating during cold weather.

Ambient Energy

Ambient energy is the energy that is all around us — for example, solar energy or wind energy. Methods of using ambient energy are often quite low-tech and low-cost. For example, an architect can design a building so that its windows face the right direction for the maximum use of daylight for both lighting and heating. That simple design feature can greatly reduce the need to use energy from other sources.

Drying wet laundry in the wind on a warm day is one of the simplest uses of ambient energy.

Even more natural energy from the Sun can be trapped if the windows are fitted with two or three layers of glass, known as double or triple glazing. Building materials themselves can also make a difference. A dark-colored brick or floor tile, for example, absorbs a lot more energy from the Sun than a pale-colored one. When the Sun goes down, the energy stored in a dark-colored brick or tile is released back into the building, keeping the temperature stable.

Energy-Saving Glass

New types of glass are making the use of ambient energy more efficient. One example is a type of double glazing that can reduce energy losses by up to 90 percent compared with standard double glazing. The technology uses a super-clear glass to allow heat and light energy from the Sun into a building. A special coating on the inside of the interior pane prevents the energy from escaping. The gap between the layers of glass is filled with argon gas. This safe and colorless gas also reduces the amount of energy passing back through the window.

Scientists are beginning to explore the possibility of capturing the ambient energy produced by humans. As people walk up and down stairs, for example, sensors built into the stairs could capture the small amounts of kinetic energy created by the pressure of human steps and convert it into electrical energy. If used in high-traffic areas, such as shopping malls, schools, or busy train stations, the combined effect could produce enough power for lighting or other low-energy uses.

 PROS: AMBIENT ENERGY

Ambient energy is free and renewable. Finding ways to use it can reduce both people's energy costs and their impact on the environment. A very simple example is hanging laundry out to dry on warm, windy days, rather than putting it in a dryer that uses electricity or natural gas. Technology to make the most of ambient energy can often be applied to existing situations. Old windows can be replaced with more efficient ones, for example, or homes can be insulated and draft proofed to prevent heat from escaping. If the technology to capture the kinetic energy of foot traffic is developed, then it could provide energy in busy places such as subways or major pedestrian walkways, which would reduce the need to use energy from less sustainable sources.

 CONS: AMBIENT ENERGY

Ambient energy such as daylight is irregular and difficult to control. On some days there can be too much and on others not enough. It can only ever be a supplement to other forms of energy, and in many northern climates, for example, it will be highly seasonal. Other forms of ambient energy, such as the wind or the energy released by people, are just as irregular and so will always require a backup. The systems to capture ambient human energy would be costly to install and may require major construction for only a very small gain in energy.

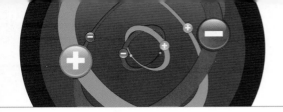

CHAPTER 5

Bioenergy and Recycled Energy

Bioenergy, also known as biomass energy or biofuel, is energy that uses biological matter from plants and animals as its source. Bioenergy is not new. People have burned wood to provide the energy for heat and cooking for thousands of years. Wood remains the main source of energy for billions of people in poorer, less-developed countries. Bioenergy can either be used raw or in a more processed form. Collecting and burning wood for energy is an example of a raw form. Wood can, however, be processed by turning it into charcoal. The benefits of charcoal are that it burns longer and hotter than wood and is much lighter to transport.

Biogas

As biological matter decomposes, or breaks down, it produces gas known as biogas. Biogas is made up of methane (typically 60 percent) and carbon dioxide (typically 40 percent). It can be collected in a sealed container called a digester for use as a fuel for cooking or heating. The biological matter used in a biogas digester is usually human or animal waste. It is fed into a large tank, which is usually buried underground. The waste must be kept at a temperature of between 86°F (30°C) and 140°F (60°C) to produce biogas, so in cooler climates the digester tank must be well insulated. The gas rises and is

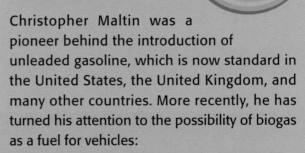

A Win-Win Situation?

VIEWPOINT

Christopher Maltin was a pioneer behind the introduction of unleaded gasoline, which is now standard in the United States, the United Kingdom, and many other countries. More recently, he has turned his attention to the possibility of biogas as a fuel for vehicles:

"Every bit of organic material on the planet eventually rots, and that methane goes up to the atmosphere. This is 21 times worse than carbon dioxide as a greenhouse gas. If you capture this methane and use it as a fuel, it is such a win-win situation. It is without doubt the most environmentally friendly fuel available to man. This is the fuel of the future."

(Christopher Maltin, Organic Power Ltd., United Kingdom)

collected in a dome at the top of the digester. A pipe out of the dome takes the gas to where it is needed. The used waste is emptied out of the digester through an outlet pipe. That waste can be used as a fertilizer to improve the soil on agricultural land.

In less-developed countries, biogas digesters are a particularly useful technology as they offer a solution to the hygienic management of waste, as well as provide a free source of energy and fertilizers. In Sri Lanka, where wood for fuel is becoming scarce and expensive, farmers use cow dung to generate biogas. The biogas provides much of the fuel needed for cooking, and the leftover solid waste is used as a fertilizer for farming. In China there are more than 7.5 million household biogas digesters and in India about 3 million. A trial project in Jinja, Uganda, has connected community toilets to a biogas digester that provides nearby homes with a regular supply of biogas. It is hoped this could be a model for many other low-income urban settlements.

This community biogas digester in Jinja, Uganda, uses waste from community toilets to produce natural gas for lighting, cooking, and heating.

Biofuel

Liquid bioenergy, or biofuel, can be used as an alternative to fossil fuels such as gasoline and diesel for powering motor vehicles. In the United Kingdom, new laws passed in 2008 mean that road fuels must contain at least 5 percent biofuels by content. That is the level considered safe for all vehicles without having to modifiy them. It is possible, however, to build vehicle engines that will use much higher levels of biofuels. Brazil is a world leader in this technology. For more than 30 years, some vehicles in Brazil have been running on ethanol fuel made entirely from sugar. Many Brazilians prefer flex-fuel cars that can run on either ethanol or gasoline, depending on which is cheaper. Gasohol, a mix of 22 percent ethanol and 78 percent gasoline, is also used as a fuel.

As oil supplies begin to run out, and as oil prices rise, more countries are considering biofuels as an alternative to oil. In the United States, ethanol production increased by almost four times between 2000 and 2007, thanks to government support for those farmers who grew crops, mainly corn, for conversion to ethanol. In 2007, about a quarter of the United States' corn crop was used for ethanol production.

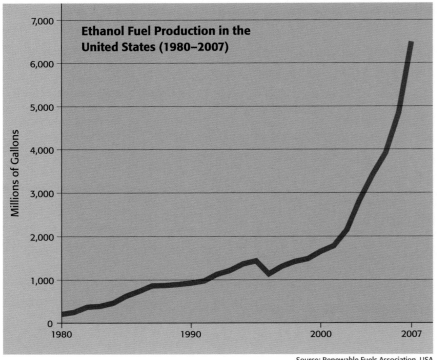

Ethanol Fuel Production in the United States (1980–2007)

Source: Renewable Fuels Association, USA

Biodiesel

Biodiesel is a substitute for diesel fuel produced from oil. It can be made from a wide variety of plants and organic wastes. The most common crops used to make biodiesel are canola and soybeans, but sunflowers, mustard, flax, and palm oil can also be used. The name biodiesel is also used for fuels that are made from a mixture of plant-based and oil-based substances. A common mix in many countries is 20 percent plant-based and 80 percent oil-based. It is also possible to make biodiesel from waste vegetable oils, such as old cooking fat from restaurants. Biodiesel can be used in many normal diesel vehicles with little modification, but in newer vehicles the engine may need to be adapted a little. Experiments with biodiesel trains and even aircraft have taken place in recent years.

A sign on this fairground ride in Maryland tells riders that it is powered by biodiesel. How useful such biofuels are for meeting our energy needs is a subject of great controversy.

SOY BIODIESEL®
Fueling Fairs, Festivals, and Fun!

Carnival Rides at this year's Montgomery County Agricultural Fair are running on clean, renewable soy-based Biodiesel fuel.
YOU can use biodiesel, too! Ask for biodiesel

Fuel or Food?

One of the greatest concerns about biofuels is whether it is a good idea to devote such a large percentage of food crops for use in fuel production, even though there are financial incentives to do so:

"Decades of declining agricultural prices have been reversed thanks to the growing use of biofuels. Farmers in some of the poorest nations have been decimated [severely affected] by U.S. and European subsidies to crops such as corn, cotton, and sugar. Today's higher prices may allow them to sell their crops at a decent price."

(Christopher Flavin, President, Worldwatch Institute)

This processing plant in South Dakota produces ethanol from corn crops. The ethanol is used either as an alternative to gasoline, or is mixed with gasoline to make blended biofuels.

PROS: BIOFUELS

Supporters of biofuels say that they use locally produced, renewable materials to create carbon-neutral energy. That means that the plants used to produce biofuels will absorb as much CO_2 during their growth as they emit when used as a fuel. No CO_2 is added to the atmosphere. Improvements in biofuel technology will increasingly allow crop wastes, such as the stubble from growing grains including rice, wheat, and corn, to be used for biofuels rather than requiring crops to be grown for fuel. That will mean farmers can earn more, by producing both a food crop and fuel crop. Biofuels have also been linked to new job opportunities. In the United States, more than 200,000 jobs have been created by the ethanol industry. In Brazil, the industry employs about 500,000 people.

CONS: BIOFUELS

Biofuel crops have been criticized for the amount of energy needed to produce them in the first place. Some scientists say that up to half of the energy in biofuels is produced using fossil fuels. In addition, the growing of crops for use as biofuels has been widely criticized for reducing the amount of crops grown for food. In 2008, a World Bank report suggested that global food prices had risen by about 75 percent since 2007 because of food crops being replaced by biofuel crops.

Recycled Energy

Vast amounts of energy are wasted around the world every day. New technologies are being developed to reduce this waste by recycling energy. In Kalundborg, Denmark, for example, heat and steam that were once wasted by the city's power station are now used by local industries, businesses, and homes. About 4,500 houses receive district heat from the power station, and a nearby oil refinery uses waste steam to heat its pipes and tanks.

Landfill Gas

Huge amounts of waste are buried in landfill sites each year. In many cases this waste contains a high level of biodegradable waste. That is waste that will break down, such as food scraps or paper. As these materials decompose they release gases — roughly 50 percent methane, 45 percent carbon dioxide, and 5 percent other gases. The technology to capture this gas and recycle it as an energy source was first used in 1975 in Palos Verdes, California. By 2006, there were about 1,150 landfill gas recovery plants worldwide. Most were in Europe, which had 730 such plants, and in the United States, which had 355. Landfill gas is either used directly as an alternative to natural gas for cooking and heating, or it can be used to power turbines to generate electricity.

 PROS: CAPTURING LANDFILL GAS

Methane gas is a major contributor to climate change. Its impact on global warming is about 21 times greater than that of carbon dioxide. Capturing landfill gas to provide energy reduces the amount of methane that is released into the atmosphere. If landfill gas is used in place of fossil fuels, it can make an even greater contribution to reducing global warming. The technology for using landfill gas as a direct fuel or to produce electricity is very similar to that used for natural gas. That means that it is relatively easy to set up at a competitive price.

CONS: CAPTURING LANDFILL GAS

Reducing the environmental impact of landfills could encourage the continued use of such sites. That is a problem, because the waste in landfill sites produces many other toxins, or poisons, and emissions besides gas. Some of those toxins can contaminate the surrounding land and water for decades. In terms of energy use, a landfill site may only produce gas for between 10 and 15 years. That can make it an expensive investment for a relatively short time. Burning landfill gas still releases carbon dioxide and other pollutants into the atmosphere.

Collecting Landfill Gas

To collect landfill gas, tunnels are drilled into the landfill site both vertically and horizontally. The tunnels allow the gas to be drawn from the landfill and collected using a network of pipes connected to a central storage tank. From there the gas is filtered to remove contaminants (mostly water vapor) that may affect its use. The gas can then be compressed so that it is ready for use as a fuel.

A landfill in Leicestershire, United Kingdom, has been fitted with pipes to extract the methane gas produced by decomposing waste. The gas powers a turbine that generates electricity.

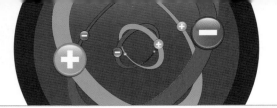

CHAPTER 6

Solar Energy

The Sun provides energy for almost all living things on Earth. Plants, for example, grow by converting radiant energy from the Sun into chemical energy — a process called photosynthesis. Every time we eat food made from plants, we are in effect eating stored solar energy. Much of the energy we use from the Sun comes to us in this stored form. Even fossil fuels are a form of solar energy that was stored by plants and animals that lived millions of years ago.

Passive Solar Energy

Passive solar energy has been used for thousands of years. One example is the use of solar energy to dry and preserve crops, meat, or fish for storage. Another is the use of greenhouses to trap the Sun's energy for

Greenhouses trap solar energy, and that speeds up the natural growth of the flowers inside.

growing plants. Buildings also benefit from passive solar energy. In the average home, about 14 percent of the heat used comes from passive solar energy through the windows and walls. Improvements in building design, such as the use of large south-facing windows and materials that better absorb heat, can make even greater use of passive solar energy and reduce energy use from other sources.

This house in Germany uses both passive and active solar energy to supply all its heating and electricity. South-facing windows and walls absorb heat from the Sun. Photovoltaic cells on the roof convert solar energy into electricity.

Active Solar Energy

When solar radiation is collected for use as an energy source, it is called active solar energy. If we were able to collect and store all the solar radiation reaching Earth in one minute, it would meet the energy needs of the world's entire population for a year! There are two main active solar technologies:

- **Solar Thermal** – Radiant energy from the Sun is used to heat a liquid contained within special tubes or panels. The heated liquid is in turn used to heat water for use in the home, or to create steam for electricity generation.
- **Solar Photovoltaic (PV)** – Electronic devices, called cells, convert the Sun's radiant energy into electricity.

How well active solar technology works depends greatly on climate and location. Both technologies are more reliable in sunnier climates, and both work best when they face the Sun for as much of the day as possible. New developments are making both technologies more efficient, however, and the use of active solar energy is growing very fast, even in less sunny regions such as northern Europe.

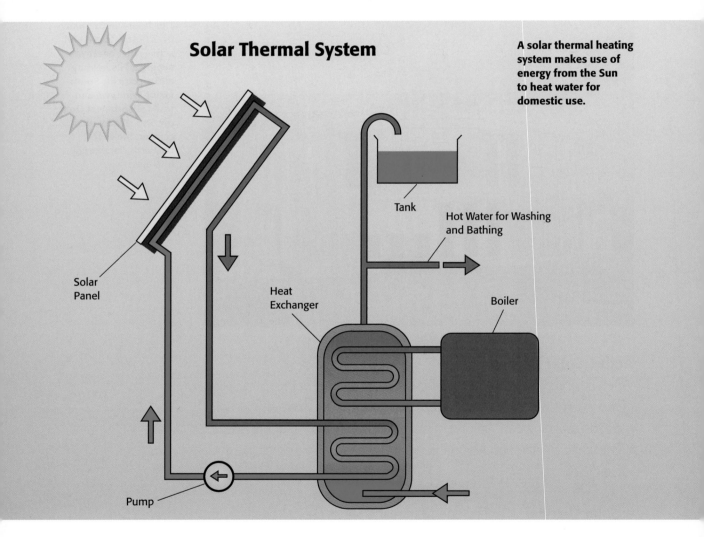

Solar Thermal System

A solar thermal heating system makes use of energy from the Sun to heat water for domestic use.

Tank

Hot Water for Washing and Bathing

Solar Panel

Heat Exchanger

Boiler

Pump

Solar Thermal

Solar thermal technology is normally used on individual buildings to provide hot water. A panel, usually mounted on the roof, contains pipes filled with liquid (typically water and antifreeze). The Sun's energy heats the liquid, which then passes through a heat exchanger to heat water for use in the building. Once the liquid has passed through the heat exchanger, it is pumped back to the panel for reheating and the cycle repeats. In sunny climates, such systems can meet nearly all the needs for hot water in an average home. However, in most cases a boiler using another fuel is also needed. A typical solar thermal system in the United States might meet one-third of all hot water needs for a home.

Energy of the Future? **VIEWPOINT**

Many people believe that solar energy is our most overlooked source of energy for the future:

"The radiation hitting the Earth is 10,000 times the consumption of energy. There is great potential in solar energy."

(José Domínguez Abascal, Chief Technology Officer at Abengoa, a Spanish Energy Company)

 PROS: SOLAR THERMAL SYSTEMS

Solar thermal systems make use of a free and renewable energy source, and produce no pollution or emissions. They are relatively simple to install, and once in place, they require little maintenance. In sunny conditions, a solar thermal system can meet almost all a household's hot water needs and reduce its energy bills considerably. These systems can be especially useful in remote areas, where other forms of energy might be less available.

 CONS: SOLAR THERMAL SYSTEMS

Solar thermal systems require a good amount of space for both the roof panels and the heat exchanger. In addition, the roof must face in the right direction and be strong enough to hold the weight of the panels. Professionally installed systems can be expensive to put in (although systems installed directly by the homeowner are cheaper). Some can take more than 20 years to pay for themselves in fuel savings. They work well on warm and clear sunny days, but will make only a small contribution to hot water in cloudy and cooler weather.

A woman drinks water from a well near Nouakchott, Mauritania. The water is pumped using energy from a solar panel. This system is ideally suited to such uses in remote areas.

Solar Photovoltaic Technology

The earliest use of photovoltaic technology was in the U.S. space program in the 1960s. At that time, PV cells were too expensive for general use and were not very efficient. Only about 4 percent of sunlight was actually converted into electricity. The most efficient experimental cells now convert

How PV Cells Work

A photovoltaic cell converts solar energy into electrical energy. It uses the photoelectric effect, a process in which electrons are emitted from some substances when they absorb energy radiated from the Sun. The most common substance used in photovoltaic cells is a semiconductor called silicon. (A semiconductor is a solid material that conducts electricity.) The silicon is specially treated so that it emits a lot of electrons to give a useful electric current.

about 40 to 50 percent of the Sun's energy, but most of the cells that are commercially available are less than 20 percent efficient. PV cells can be used on their own to power items such as watches or calculators, but where more power is needed, several are put together as a PV module. For even greater power, PV modules are joined to form a PV array, often called a solar panel.

Some of the most advanced solar power technology continues to be used in space exploration, where no other energy sources are available. The International Space Station (ISS) is powered by high-tech PV cells, as are many satellites. On Earth, engineers are experimenting with using PV cells to power vehicles. At the moment, however, this technology is limited to one-off demonstration cars and is not yet commercially possible.

 PROS: PHOTOVOLTAIC SYSTEMS

Photovoltaic systems can generate electricity even during dull weather and are an inexpensive and efficient source of electricity for homes that are not connected to a national power grid. They have been widely used to provide electricity in less-developed countries, for example. PV cells produce no emissions, and because they have no moving parts, there is very little to go wrong or maintain. Improvements in the efficiency of PV systems and new PV materials are lowering the costs of PV technology every year.

 CONS: PHOTOVOLTAIC SYSTEMS

Solar PV has a high initial cost, and a typical household system may take more than 25 years (about the same as its lifetime) to pay for itself in energy savings. Specialist knowledge is needed to fit a PV system, and its location must be correct to work most efficiently. PV cells do not generate electricity during the night and will produce less in cloudy conditions. That means additional sources of electricity are needed to back up the use of solar PV.

Concentrated Solar Power

The Sun's energy is very spread out when it reaches the surface of Earth. Scientists are developing methods to gather this energy using concentrated solar power (CSP) technologies. All the various CSP technologies use the same principle of reflecting sunlight off mirrors, called heliostats, onto a single collection point. The intense heat created at the collection point is used to produce superheated steam. The steam drives a turbine to generate electricity. The United States and Spain are world leaders in CSP technology and already have several operating plants. In California, CSP plants produced enough electricity for 350,000 homes in 2008. In Spain, a new solar tower CSP plant called PS20 opened in 2009 near Seville. It produces enough electricity for 11,000 homes and is the world's largest CSP plant to provide electricity to a national grid, the network that supplies a country's electricity. Spain plans to build 50 more CSP plants by 2015 and is exporting its solar power technology to Morocco, Algeria, and the United States.

Solar Tower

A solar tower works by using hundreds of large mirrors called heliostats to focus the Sun's rays onto a single collection point. This creates a very high temperature that is used to produce superheated steam that is then passed through a turbine to generate electricity. Engineers are developing new systems to enable solar towers to generate electricity during cloudy weather and even at night. This is done by using energy captured during the day to heat up molten salts that are kept in storage tanks. Molten salt is used because it stores heat better than water does. At night, the hot salt becomes a source of heat that continues driving the turbines.

This solar tower is located near Seville, Spain. The field of heliostats concentrate the Sun's energy onto the tower and can be seen around its base.

PROS: CONCENTRATED SOLAR POWER

Concentrated solar power systems are the cheapest way to convert sunlight into electricity, and they can supply significant amounts of power to a national grid. CSP is also a proven technology that has been generating electricity in the United States since 1984. In places that are far from a national grid, CSP can be used locally to power a small settlement or factory, for example. As the technology develops, its cost is becoming more affordable. Power from CSP systems could soon be as cheap as electricity produced using natural gas or coal.

 CONS: CONCENTRATED SOLAR POWER

Concentrated solar power systems can work only where there is a guaranteed supply of sunlight and plenty of space to locate the many mirrors that are needed. Each of the 1,000 heliostats used for Spain's PS20 solar tower is half the size of a tennis court. The initial building cost is high, and the technology requires specialized knowledge and equipment. CSP systems can't generate electricity at night and so must be used alongside other systems.

CSP Technology in Deserts

 **VIEWPOINT**

Trials with CSP technology suggest it could work very well in desert regions with plenty of sunlight. One company specializing in generating power in deserts explains why:

"Every year, each square kilometer of desert receives solar energy equivalent to 1.5 million barrels of oil. Multiplying by the area of deserts worldwide, this is several hundred times the entire current energy consumption of the world. Using CSP, less than 1 percent of the world's deserts could generate as much electricity as the world is now using."

(A representatives from Desertec, an company specializing in solar energy)

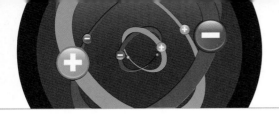

CHAPTER 7

Wind Energy

Energy has been harnessed from the wind for centuries. The earliest windmills were used in ancient Persia to grind grain or pump water in the A.D. 600s. The first windmill to generate electricity was built in 1888 by Charles F. Brush in Cleveland, Ohio, but the idea did not become widely popular. In the twentieth century, Denmark became the center of developments in wind energy. It was there that the first modern turbine, called the Gedser turbine, was built in 1957. Since then, the design of turbines has changed relatively little, although new materials and computer-controlled design and operation have allowed turbines to become bigger and more powerful. Today's modern wind turbines produce up to 30 times more electricity than the Gedser turbine of 1957!

A Global Industry

Wind power is one of the fastest-growing methods of producing energy in the world. There are many reasons for the increasing interest in wind energy, including improvements in efficiency, lower construction costs, and the fact that it is relatively easy to install a wind turbine. The United States and Europe still dominate the global wind industry, but the technology is now spreading to other parts of the world, especially China and India. China has set targets to produce enough electricity from wind power to meet the needs of about 10 million households by 2020.

Worldwide Growth in Wind Power, 1996–2007 (in megawatts, MW)	
1996	6,100
1997	7,600
1998	10,200
1999	13,600
2000	17,400
2001	23,900
2002	31,100
2003	39,341
2004	47,620
2005	59,084
2006	74,051
2007	93,864

Source: Global Wind Energy Council

Modern Wind Turbines

Most modern turbines are of a standard design, which has helped reduce their cost dramatically. They normally have three rotor blades, which are attached to a central hub. The hub is connected to the structure that houses all the generating equipment, called the nacelle. Inside the nacelle are the mechanisms that convert kinetic energy into electrical energy. The nacelle also includes systems that monitor conditions to make maximum use of the available wind. The systems can shut down the turbine in high winds to prevent damage. The nacelle is located on a tower that lifts the entire mechanism high in the air. That enables the rotor blades to turn freely.

Coasts are ideal locations for wind farms as they are free from obstacles that can cause turbulence. However, coasts may also be popular for tourism, so the placement of wind farms in those locations can be controversial.

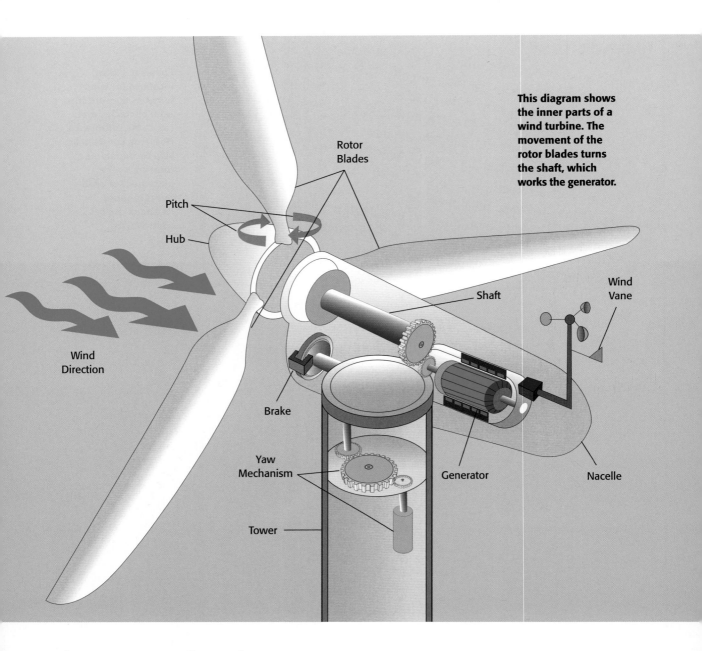

Rotor
Blades

This diagram shows the inner parts of a wind turbine. The movement of the rotor blades turns the shaft, which works the generator.

Pitch

Hub

Shaft

Wind Vane

Wind Direction

Brake

Yaw Mechanism

Generator

Nacelle

Tower

The Importance of Location

Wind varies not only in direction and speed but also according to location. Wind speeds tend to be faster at high altitudes and at the coast, for example. That is because the wind meets less resistance from obstacles such as trees, buildings, and hills. Even the smoothness of the landscape (how rocky it is, for example) makes a difference to the potential wind energy available.

When the flow of wind is disrupted by being deflected around or through a particular obstacle, it creates turbulence. Turbulence is a major consideration when situating wind turbines. Turbulence slows wind speeds or creates uneven and irregular patterns, both of which reduce the efficiency of turbines. Turbulence can extend up to three times the height of the obstacle, so a house that is 39 feet (12 meters) tall can disrupt the flow of wind for up to 117 feet (36 meters) around it. That is why wind farms, as collections of individual turbines are called, are often located in open, exposed areas on hills or on coasts, away from any obstacles.

The Antiwind Lobby

Wind turbines, possibly more than any other renewable energy source, attract very strong opinions from people who live near them. There are complaints about them ruining landscapes and making too much noise. Some conservationists claim they are a danger to birds and disturb other wildlife. Supporters of wind turbines say that such claims are weak and that studies show they are a relatively harmless technology that causes very little disruption to people living nearby. The background noise of cars or the wind is often louder than a modern turbine, for example. Nevertheless, plans for new wind turbines frequently meet with objections from local residents, and this can slow the spread of the technology.

Coping With Wind

To make the most of wind energy, scientists have developed various technologies that are now built into modern wind turbines. The two most important are the yaw and blade pitch mechanisms:

● **Yaw Mechanism** — This is a system of gears and motors located between the nacelle and tower and connected by electronic sensors to a wind vane. When the vane detects a change in wind direction, the yaw mechanism turns the nacelle to face the wind. A turbine is most efficient when it is perpendicular, or at a right angle, to the oncoming wind.

● **Blade Pitch Mechanism** — This system controls the pitch, or angle, of the rotor blades. In lower wind speeds the blades are pitched into the wind. That means they are made flatter, or more vertical, to catch more energy. In higher wind speeds the blades can be pitched out of the wind, or turned more horizontal, to slow or completely stop the turbine. This system also acts as a safety mechanism to protect the rotor blades during very strong winds.

Offshore Wind Power

Scientists have known for many years that the best conditions for generating wind energy are at sea. However, building turbines out at sea is more expensive than locating them on land. Establishing the turbine foundations on the seabed and raising the towers on top requires expensive and specialized equipment. The turbines and the cables on the seabed must be strong enough to withstand the force of the waves and the corrosive effects of salt water. Denmark has been developing offshore wind farms since the early 1990s, but such farms have only recently become a popular and more widespread technology. That is mainly due to improvements in foundation construction and because larger and more powerful turbines make each foundation more cost-effective.

 PROS: OFFSHORE WIND FARMS

Larger offshore wind turbines could reduce the cost of wind energy in the long term and, because there is more wind and less turbulence at sea, offshore turbines are more reliable and have a longer lifespan than land-based turbines. Locating turbines offshore avoids spoiling landscapes and reduces the visual and noise impact for people living nearby.

 CONS: OFFSHORE WIND FARMS

Offshore wind turbines still have a high cost of installation compared with land-based turbines. Some people object to them on the grounds that they spoil coastal views. There are concerns that the technology is unproven and may not last as long as hoped. Installation and maintenance at sea is dangerous, and there are not enough specialized boats and engineers to meet the targets being set by some governments. There are also concerns about the danger to shipping and to marine wildlife, including seabirds. Ultimately this is a technology that can only generate electricity when the wind is blowing — and only as long as it isn't blowing too strong!

This specialized ship is used to install offshore wind turbines. The large legs sticking in the air are used to raise the ship out of the water once it reaches the installation site. The technical difficulties and costs of turbine installation mean that offshore wind remains an expensive option.

Offshore Wind — Good or Bad?

VIEWPOINT

Offshore wind is a proven technology, but there are doubts about its potential. Wind farms may have a negative impact on wildlife and pose a hazard to existing radar systems:

"Cape Wind's proposal to build America's first offshore wind farm on Horseshoe Shoal would provide three-quarters of the electricity used on Cape Cod from clean, renewable energy .... Cape Wind will create new jobs, stabilize electricity costs, increase energy independence, and establish Massachusetts as a leader in offshore wind power."

(Jim Gordon, CEO and Project Developer for Cape Wind)

"The Federal Aviation Administration [FAA] has found potential for physical and/or electromagnetic interference to the radar systems used by the FAA .... and has issued a 'presumed hazard' determination for Cape Wind because of its potential impact to the 400,000 flights per year that travel over the proposed project."

(Representative from the U.S. Federal Aviation Administration)

CHAPTER 8

Water Energy

The power of flowing water has long been used to turn wheels in water mills. The mechanical energy created by the movement of the wheel was put to many uses — for example, to grind grain or saw wood. Water energy was first used to generate electricity in 1882 in Wisconsin. Today, electricity produced by water power, called hydroelectric power (HEP), is a major energy source in many countries.

The Hoover Dam on the Nevada-Arizona border holds back the waters of the Colorado River. The pressure of the water retained behind the dam wall is used to generate clean, renewable energy.

Hydroelectric Power

The amount of energy available from water depends on its flow. Many HEP systems use dams to hold back water in a reservoir. When electricity is needed, a gate to a large pipe called the penstock is opened in the dam. Water flows rapidly through the penstock and hits the turbine blades, causing them to turn. A shaft connects the spinning turbine to a generator that produces an electrical current. The current is distributed through power lines to a national grid.

A Question of Scale

Large HEP systems provide a clean, reliable, and renewable source of energy. They can, however, be controversial because of their impact on both people and the environment. The Three Gorges Dam on the Chang River in China, for example, was completed in 2008 and will provide electricity equivalent to 15 large coal-fired power stations by 2011. Nevertheless, there have been many criticisms of this project. The reservoir created by the dam has flooded 244 square miles (632 sq. km) of land and has forced more than a million people to move to new homes. There are also concerns about water quality in the reservoir, because the dam traps pollutants released from surrounding towns and industries, as well as from factories and homes that now lie underwater.

 PROS: LARGE-SCALE HYDROELECTRIC POWER SYSTEMS

Large dams can provide low-cost renewable energy and replace the use of more polluting energy sources such as coal or oil. The price of electricity produced by HEP dams is reasonably stable as it does not depend on changing supplies of fuel. That can make HEP systems a good source of energy for lower-income countries. Low-cost energy also helps support the development of industries.

 CONS: LARGE-SCALE HYDROELECTRIC POWER SYSTEMS

Critics of large-scale HEP systems say that similar amounts of energy can be generated by many smaller dams. These small-scale HEP systems do not have the wide-ranging social and environmental impacts of a large project such as the Three Gorges Dam. Large-scale systems can disrupt entire river systems. For example, there are several rivers, including the Nile in Egypt and the Colorado River in the United States, that no longer reach the sea during parts of the year because of disruption caused by large dams. That can reduce the water for settlements downstream and for farming. It can also have a devastating effect on wildlife.

Micro-Hydroelectric Power

Many people consider small HEP projects, called micro-hydro systems, to be more sustainable than large HEP projects. Micro-hydro systems work in a similar way by diverting water through a penstock and turbine to drive a generator and produce electricity. The difference with micro-hydro systems is that they can mostly be used without the need for a dam. They simply divert part of the regular flow of a river through the turbine before returning it directly to the river. That means there is much less disruption to the natural flow of the river and the wildlife that depends upon it.

Where dams are used, they are much smaller than in larger systems and, in many cases, have only minimal impacts. Improvements in the efficiency of turbines have enabled micro-hydro technology to become smaller and cheaper. There are even hopes that it could one day use the pressure of water flowing through household plumbing systems to generate electricity each time you turn on the faucet!

A micro-HEP turbine installed on the slopes of Mount Kenya in Kenya uses water diverted from the Kabiri Falls to generate electricity for local use. Similar systems could meet small-scale energy needs in many locations around the world.

Good for the Environment?

The environmental impact of large-scale HEP is one of the major reasons that small-scale hydropower is considered better by leading energy scientists:

"Micro-hydro, or small-scale hydro, is one of the most environmentally benign energy conversion options available, because unlike large-scale hydropower, it does not attempt to interfere significantly with river flows."

(Peter Fraenkel, Founder and Technical Director of Marine Current Turbines Ltd., Bristol, United Kingdom)

 PROS: MICRO-HYDROELECTRIC SYSTEMS

Because of their smaller scale, micro-hydroelectric systems can be used in many locations and do not require lengthy and technical construction work to become operational. A well-designed system can have minimal impact on the local environment while still providing a source of clean and renewable energy. The efficiency of a micro-hydro system can be as high as 90 percent, compared with about 30 to 40 percent for many solar- or wind-power alternatives. Micro-hydro is especially suited to remote regions where connection to a national grid might be difficult or expensive.

 CONS: MICRO-HYDROELECTRIC SYSTEMS

Micro-hydroelectric systems can stop working in periods of low water flow and may have strong seasonal fluctuations unless a small dam is used to store water for dry season use. The initial cost of a micro-hydro system can be too high to make it an affordable option for individual users. In addition, some of the energy produced may be wasted unless an electrical storage system, such as batteries, is installed.

Tidal Power

The power of tides and waves can also be used to generate HEP, although these technologies are less developed than using dams. Tidal systems use the energy of falling and rising tides to generate electricity by forcing the moving water through turbines. The turbines are housed in a barrage, the name for a barrier that is built across water. The Rance tidal barrage in France, which opened in 1966, was the first active tidal HEP plant in the world. In this barrage, the turbines are contained in a solid wall, like a dam, that lies across an estuary. An alternative to a complete barrage is a tidal fence, which is a line of submerged turbines with gaps between to allow for the passage of ships or wildlife. Proposals for tidal fences have been made for the Severn estuary in the United Kingdom and for the San Bernardino Strait in the Philippines. Tidal fences and barrages are extremely expensive to build and face criticism from environmentalists for their likely disruption to wildlife and habitats.

A more viable tidal technology is the tidal turbine, which could operate as an individual unit or in small turbine farms, much like wind farms. Some experimental tidal turbines are already in operation; for example,

The tidal barrage on the river Rance in France is one of the few existing systems that use tidal energy to generate electricity. However, several new barrages are now either in planning or under construction around the world.

a turbine in Strangford Lough, Northern Ireland, generates enough electricity for 1,000 homes. In the United States, the first phase of a tidal turbine project for the East River between Manhattan and Queens in New York City was completed in 2006. That project will eventually use up to 300 small tidal turbines, completely submerged beneath the river, to provide electricity for about 8,000 homes.

How Tidal Turbines Work

A tidal turbine works much like a wind turbine, but with the rotors submerged under the sea to catch the force of the tidal current. Water is about 800 times denser than air, so ocean currents contain much higher levels of energy than wind currents. That means tidal turbines can use smaller and slower-turning rotor blades to generate the same amount of energy as larger wind turbines.

PROS: TIDAL TURBINES

Tidal turbines provide a more regular and eventually cheaper source of renewable energy than wind or solar sources. They can be used in any location with a reasonable and regular tidal current and are relatively cheap to manufacture and install. Because they are positioned in the water rather than in a barrage across it, they do not disrupt shipping or the migration of wildlife. The rotors turn relatively slowly (about 10 times slower than a ship's propeller) and so should not disrupt marine life.

CONS: TIDAL TURBINES

The electricity produced by tidal turbines is currently more expensive than from many other sources, and the technology only benefits regions or countries with suitable tidal currents. Individual turbines are not yet as powerful as offshore wind turbines, producing only about a quarter of the electricity of wind turbines. The planned larger tidal turbine farms could disturb or displace fishing close to the shore. Some people are also concerned about whether the technology can survive difficult conditions at sea.

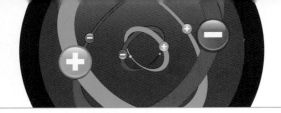

CHAPTER 9

Future Energy Sources

If current predictions about energy supplies are correct, we will begin to run out of fossil fuels at some point in the middle of this century. That concern, combined with growing worries about the effect our reliance on fossil fuels is having on the environment, is leading to a rush to find new sources of energy for the future.

Some of the technologies, such as using the power of ocean currents for tidal turbines, are real possibilities. All they need is to become more cost-effective or for governments to provide support to help them become established. Other ideas, such as beaming solar power from space or wind turbines that float high in the air where wind currents are stronger, are perhaps more extreme. Still, that is not stopping scientists from working on such projects and many others.

Daunting Challenge

The challenge for any future technology will be to provide energy at an affordable price and in large enough quantities to meet growing global energy demands. There are millions of people who do not have access to enough energy today. Any future technology needs not

Solar Power From Space

Scientists have been planning to use space solar power (SSP) as an energy source since the 1960s, but the technology has yet to take off. The idea is to send giant collectors and photovoltaic cells into space, where they would orbit Earth. The cells would convert energy from the Sun into an electrical current, in much the same way PV cells do on Earth. The benefit of SSP is that sunlight is about eight times more powerful in space than on Earth – and available all the time. The electrical current would be converted into microwaves and beamed to Earth, where it would be converted back into electrical current for a national grid. Alternatively, the Japanese space agency, JAXA, has developed a system that would use a laser beam to send the current to Earth. It hopes to have a system capable of powering half a million homes up and running by 2030.

merely to replace existing energy sources, but also to make energy available to everyone. Some of this can be achieved through improvements in efficiency, allowing the same energy sources to be used more wisely, but new technologies will have to play their part, too.

Will energy one day be transmitted back to Earth from solar satellites like this? That is the hope of various scientific teams that intend to use lasers or microwaves to convert the near-endless solar energy in space into clean, renewable energy on Earth.

A Hydrogen Economy

Hydrogen is a potential energy source that is all around us. However, it requires capturing and processing before it becomes usable. Water is made of hydrogen and oxygen. Hydrogen can be separated from water by passing an electrical current through water to split it into hydrogen and oxygen. That process is called electrolysis. Hydrocarbons (hydrogen and carbon) are found in most fuels, and hydrogen can be extracted from natural gas. To create an energy source, the hydrogen is pumped into hydrogen fuel cells. Those special cells combine hydrogen with oxygen, causing a chemical reaction inside each cell that produces heat, an electrical current, and water. Both the heat and electricity can be used. The only waste from a hydrogen fuel cell is water.

 PROS: HYDROGEN FUEL CELLS

Hydrogen fuel cells can be adapted for use in vehicles, homes, and power stations. That makes it a possible technology to replace many existing energy sources. It is also a more concentrated source of energy than oil. Improvements in hydrogen storage and transportation could make it possible to use a network similar to existing oil and gas networks to deliver clean energy to homes around the world. The process of electrolysis requires electricity. If energy from renewable sources such as solar, wind, or geothermal were used to power this process, then it could be a highly sustainable technology.

 CONS: HYDROGEN FUEL CELLS

Hydrogen is not naturally occurring in our environment. It is locked up in water with oxygen or in hydrocarbons with carbon. Separating hydrogen is an energy-intensive process. At the moment, hydrogen fuel cells are competing with other, cheaper technologies, and there is still more research to do. Governments have begun to fund these programs, but much more investment is needed if a hydrogen economy is to become a reality.

A hydrogen-powered bus in Reykjavík, Iceland, runs on electricity produced by a hydrogen fuel cell. There are hopes that hydrogen could be the fuel of the future and replace the role of oil in our lives.

A Hydrogen Future?

VIEWPOINT

The possibility of a world powered by hydrogen has excited many experts around the world, but there are others who caution that it may not be the answer to the world's energy problems:

"Our vision is that when we have transformed Iceland into a hydrogen economy, then we are completely independent of imported fossil fuel. There will be no greenhouse gas emissions from our fuel."

(Bragi Árnason, Professor of Chemistry, University of Iceland, Reykjavík, Iceland)

"The advantages of hydrogen praised by journalists … are misleading, because the production of hydrogen depends on the availability of energy and water, both of which are increasingly rare and may become political issues, as much as oil and natural gas are today."

(Dr. Ulf Bossel, Engineer, European Fuel Cell Forum)

GLOSSARY

altitude Height above sea level

atom The smallest part of an element

biofuel A fuel derived from organic matter

biogas A gas made from decomposing organic plant and animal matter

biomass Organic matter, such as plants or animals

bitumen A sticky hydrocarbon derived from petroleum and found naturally in some sands and rocks; bitumen can be processed into oil

carbon A nonmetallic chemical element that combines with other elements to form the basis of living organisms

carbon neutral Not emitting carbon, or compensating for carbon emitted by absorbing an equal amount of carbon

chain reaction When one reaction causes another, which in turn causes another, and so on; the basis for the creation of nuclear energy, as the splitting of one atom begins the process of the splitting other atoms

coal A type of rock formed from the decomposition of plant and animal material; coal is normally black or brown in color and used as a fuel

combustion The process of a material reacting with oxygen to produce energy in the form of heat and flames

concentrated When something has a high density of a common element

decompose To break down organic matter

district heating A system in which heating is provided from a common system in a district instead of individual systems for each property

electrolysis The passing of electricity through a liquid in order to separate it into its component parts; for example, to separate water into hydrogen and oxygen

electron A negatively charged stable particle that surrounds the nucleus, or center, of an atom

emission A discharge from a process or material

ethanol A colorless liquid produced by fermenting organic plant matter that can be used as a fuel alternative to gasoline

fission The process of splitting an atom to release the energy holding it together

fossil fuel A fuel that is made up of the decomposed organic remains of plants and animals; oil, natural gas, and coal

fuel cell A mechanism that produces energy by combining elements to create a reaction; fuel cells combine hydrogen with oxygen to release energy and water

fusion The process of fusing, or joining, atoms to release energy

gasoline A fuel derived from oil that is commonly used to power motor vehicles

geothermal Energy from Earth

global warming The process by which the average temperatures of the near-Earth atmosphere and Earth's surface are gradually rising

greenhouse gas Any gas, including water vapor, that acts like a greenhouse when released into the atmosphere by trapping energy from the Sun close to Earth's surface

heat exchanger A mechanism for transferring energy from one substance, normally a liquid or gas, to another for the purpose of heating or cooling

hydroelectric Describes the generation of electricity by transferring the kinetic energy of moving water

Industrial Revolution A period that began in the late 18th century in Britain in which there was rapid development of industrial technology and increased use of energy from fossil fuels

kinetic energy The energy of motion, such as the motion of waves, molecules, or objects

landfill A site used to bury wastes

laser A highly concentrated and focused beam of electromagnetic energy

megawatt (MW) A unit of power equal to 1 million watts

methane A gas produced as organic plant and animal matter decomposes; methane is a major greenhouse gas, but it can be captured for use as a source of energy (biogas)

microwave A type of electromagnetic energy wave that is used in cooking and communications

nacelle The unit at the top of a wind turbine that contains the mechanical parts and connects to the turbine blades

national grid A network of electricity distribution that covers most or all of a country and is fed by a variety of power sources

neutron A subatomic particle that has no electrical charge

nuclear Relating to the use of atomic energy for generating electricity; also associated with atomic energy used for weapons

oil A liquid fossil fuel made from decomposed organic plant and animal matter

photovoltaic (PV) Describes the ability to generate electricity when exposed to sunlight

pitch The angle of a wind turbine blade against the wind; the blade can be pitched into the wind (flat against it to create more force) or out of it (sideways to let the wind flow over it)

plutonium A toxic and radioactive silvery metallic chemical that is found in some uranium ores and also generated as nuclear waste

pollutant Any substance that contaminates an environment

potential energy Stored energy that has the possibility of releasing energy

radiant energy Electromagnetic energy that travels in waves and includes visible light (solar energy), X-rays, and radio waves

radiation Energy emitted from unstable elements such as plutonium or uranium and that can be highly damaging to people and animals; radioactive describes unstable elements such as plutonium or uranium that emit radiation

GLOSSARY

reactor A mechanism that enables the controlled reaction of atoms to create nuclear energy

renewable Something with the ability to be renewed; describes solar or wind energy that will not run out

semiconductor A solid material that has a limited ability to conduct electricity

solar Relating to the Sun; energy from the Sun

superheated Describes a substance that has been heated to a highly volatile state so that it contains a great amount of potential energy

sustainable Using resources in such a way that there is no long-term damage to the environment

tar sands Naturally occurring sands that contain a high volume of bitumen that could be processed for use as oil

thermal energy The internal energy in a substance created by movement and released as heat

turbine A mechanical device that converts energy from one form, such as moving wind, water, or steam, into another form, such as electricity

turbulence An unstable and irregular pattern of movement, normally in relation to wind or water

uranium A heavy, silver-white metallic chemical that is highly radioactive and can be used as a fuel for producing nuclear energy

vapor The gaseous state of a substance

voltage Used to describe electrical potential energy

watt (W) A unit of power equal to one joule of energy per second

yaw To turn around a vertical axis; for example, a wind turbine has a yaw mechanism on top of the support tower that can turn it into or out of the wind

FURTHER INFORMATION

WEB SITES

The Ecologist
www.theecologist.org/energy/index.asp
The web site of *The Ecologist* features regular sections devoted to innovations in energy.

Energy Information Administration (EIA)
www.eia.doe.gov/kids/energyfacts/sources/ renewable/renewable.html
The EIA web site reports information about the future role of renewable energy in the United States and includes graphs, statistics, and a slide show.

New Scientist
www.newscientist.com
The *New Scientist* web site reports breakthroughs and discoveries in energy and technology.

PBS.org
Lesson Plan: Global Warming
www.pbs.org/now/classroom/globalwarming.html
The web site of the PBS news program *NOW* offers a detailed web site for students that explains how greenhouse gasses are increasing temperatures on Earth and what we can expect form climate change.

Scientific American
www.sciam.com/energy
The energy section of the U.S. science magazine *Scientific American* offers current information about energy alternatives.

U.S. Department of Energy
www.energy.gov/forstudentsandkids.htm
The U.S. Department of Energy site for students provides information and activities that explain and compare different energy sources.

World Without Oil
worldwithoutoil.org/metastudents.htm
World Without Oil offers a series of lessons for students to help them foster an understanding of our dependence on fossil fuels and what to expect as oil supplies reach their peak.

BOOKS

Ballard, Carol. *From Steam Engines to Nuclear Fusion: Discovering Energy*. Heinemann (2008)

Cartlidge, Cherese. *Ripped from the Headlines – The Environment: Alternative Energy*. Erickson Press (2008)

Kent, Peter. *Navigators: Technology*. Kingfisher (2009)

Kerr Casper, Julie. *Natural Resources: Energy*. Chelsea House Publishers (2007)

Langwith, Jacqueline. *Opposing Viewpoints: Renewable Energy*. Greenhaven Press (2008)

Laxer, James. *Oil*. Groundwood Books (2008)

Leone, Daniel. *At Issue: Is the World Heading Toward an Energy Crisis?* Greenhaven Press (2005)

Morgan, Sally. *Chain Reactions: From Windmills to Hydrogen Fuel Cells*. Heinemann (2007)

Olwell, Russell B. *The International Atomic Energy Agency*. Chelsea House Publishers (2008)

Oxlade, Chris. *New Technology: Energy Technology*. Heinemann (2008)

Rooney, Anne. *Solar Power*. Gareth Stevens Publishing (2008)

Sherman, Jill. *Essential Viewpoints: Oil and Energy Alternatives*. Essential Library (2008)

Snedden, Robert. *Essential Energy: Energy Alternatives*. Heinemann (2006)

INDEX

Page numbers in **BOLD** refer to illustrations and charts.

About the Author
Rob Bowden is a freelance author and photographer specializing in environmental and developmental issues. He has written more than 70 children's books and has traveled widely in Africa, Europe, and Asia.

About the Consultant
Dr. Robert Fairbrother is a Visiting Senior Lecturer at King's College, University of London. A science teacher, he was awarded honorary membership to the Association for Science Education in recognition of his services to science education.